Getting Confirmed:
A Journey of Questions and Answers

Contents

Published by
Redemptorist Publications
Alphonsus House Chawton Alton Hampshire GU34 3HQ.

Copyright © The Congregation of the Most Holy Redeemer.
A Registered Charity.

First Printing   September 1995

Text by: Steven J Givens
Design by: Roger Smith

Photographs: Image Bank. Cover: Black male; Pages; 2 & 3; 8; 9; 14 &15
Zefa Pictures. Cover: Girl; Picnic scene; Pages: 2 Girl; 5; 6 & 7; 10 & 11
David Toase: Pages 12 & 13

Printed by: Knight & Willson Limited, Leeds, LS11 5SF

Nihil Obstat: Cyril Murtagh V.G.
Censor Deputatus
Imprimatur † Crispian Hollis
Episcopus Portus Magni
Portus Magni, August 1995

The Nihil Obstat and Imprimatur are a declaration that a book or pamphlet is considered to be free from doctrinal or moral error. It is not implied that those who have granted the Nihil Obstat and Imprimatur agree with the contents, opinions and statements expressed.

ISBN 0 85231 153 2

Welcome to the Club

Let's say there was a club to which you really, really wanted to belong. What would you be willing to do to get into that club?

Would you go to the meetings, learn the rules, learn about the history of the club and even study to take a test in order to get in? Would you be willing to be "initiated" by those already in the club? Or maybe it's a team you'd like to be on. Would you be willing to run the miles, do the exercises, go through the drills and learn the plays in order to be a part of the team?
If the club or the team is important enough to you, your answer to all these questions would be an enthusiastic "Yes!" Many of you have already been through the rigours of joining a new club or trying out for the team. So you know that all the hard work can be worth it.

Sometimes when you want to join a new club you have to be sponsored by someone who is already a member. They must bring you to the meetings, introduce you to the members and help you on your way to learning the rules of the club so you can become a full member. Without them you would never get to be a member.

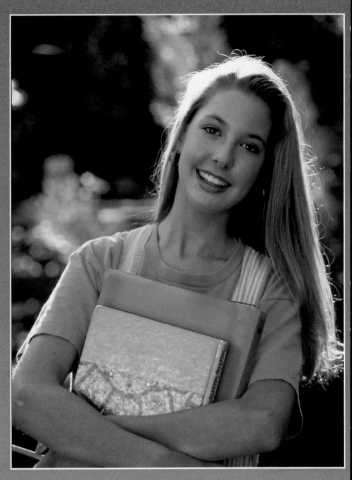

Okay, you know this book is not about joining clubs or making the team. Or is it? For as you begin your journey toward receiving the Sacrament of Confirmation, you are embarking on a journey that will complete your initiation into one of the largest clubs in the world – the Church. In receiving this Sacrament you are accepting God's gift, you are fully united with God through the Holy Spirit in the life and work of his Church.

Your Journey up to Now

When you were a baby you were presented to the Church by your parents and your baptismal sponsors – your Godparents. They did this

because they wanted to share a gift with you as soon as they could – the gift of the Christian faith. Then – slowly – you started to learn the lifestyle of the Church and attended church with your family. You learned simple prayers like the "Our Father" and the "Sign of the Cross."

As you grew older you learned many more things about what being a Christian really means. You began to participate in the wonderful gifts that God and the Church have given us in the sacraments. You received your first communion and began to participate weekly in the celebration of the Eucharist. You went to confession and received the Sacrament of Reconciliation so you could come to terms with the ways in which you turn away from God and reject his life of love. You learned the history of the Church and about the sacred scriptures and the writings of the Church fathers.

In short, you learned what it means to be a Christian. You learned what it takes to be a member of the club. Now, finally, the time is approaching when you get to decide for yourself whether or not this club is for you. God offers you the gift of being called to be part of the work of his Church. Are your hands open, are you willing to receive this gift?

Standing On Your Own

According to the Church you have reached the "age of reason." You are now old enough and wise enough to speak up for yourself, saying with your own voice the words your parents and Godparents said for you long ago.

With this sacrament you will become a full member of the Church – as much a member as your parents or anyone else in your parish or in Christian churches around the world. You become a real part of God's worldwide Church – not a member because your parents are members, but a member because that's what you choose to do. That's a big difference, and that's why Confirmation is such a big deal. In the eyes of the Church, you are an adult once you are confirmed.

That's also why right now you should have a lot of questions about your faith and your Church. And you should be wondering about what this "Confirmation thing" is all about. That's why this book was written – to give you straight answers about this important next step in your Christian journey. This is a journey you have already begun, it is a journey which will continue for the rest of your life.

That was your first question, wasn't it? Or maybe it was this: "If it's my decision then why are my parents making me go?" They're both good questions and deserve good, truthful answers.

Your parents are encouraging – or even making – you go to Confirmation classes because they want you to share fully in the Church. They want you to be their equal in the Church. Perhaps more importantly, your parents care deeply for you and your faith – your relationship with God. So although there may be a bit of "pushing" on their part to get you to Confirmation classes, they're doing it because they care.

Part of being confirmed and becoming an adult in the eyes of the Church is accepting the responsibility that comes with your full membership. That's what your parents are doing. When they married they promised to "accept children lovingly from God and bring them up according to the law of Christ and his Church." They are bound by that promise to pass their faith on to you, and part of that is seeing you through to full membership in the Church. So your willingness to be confirmed is also helping your parents fulfill a very important promise they made to each other, to the Church, and to God.

Full members of the Church are respectful of others and of what the Church asks us to do to nurture our faith.

Finally, and perhaps most importantly, you need Confirmation because it's one of the most important statements you'll ever make about yourself. There's nothing magic about "going through" Confirmation unless you have made a personal decision to approach the sacrament with honesty and faith. The Sacrament of Confirmation is nothing without you. It requires your response. Your preparation for the sacrament will lead you to the point where you can honestly make that decision. After that, it's all up to you.

First Question:

Why Do I Need to Do This?

Who Started All This?

In a word, God.

When Jesus was baptized by his cousin, John the Baptist, the Holy Sprit came down out of the sky as a dove and rested on Jesus, symbolizing that Jesus was the Messiah. So the Holy Spirit "confirmed" Jesus' baptism by John, just as your Confirmation will "confirm" your baptism.

Here was a visible sign that Jesus lived his life in communion with the Holy Spirit. But Jesus, in turn, told his disciples that the Holy Spirit was not just for him. The Spirit was for everyone, and Jesus promised his disciples that the Holy Spirit would come to them after Jesus left earth to go back up to heaven to be with the Father.

Jesus fulfilled this promise on the day of Pentecost, when the Holy Spirit, like a mighty wind, rushed into the room where the disciples were gathered and settled on their heads like tongues of fire. Filled with this Spirit, the disciples began to proclaim the mighty works of God. Those who heard and believed what the disciples were saying were baptized and then "confirmed" when the Holy Spirit came to them also.

From that day on, the apostles would "lay their hands" on new Christians to give them the gift of the Holy Spirit and confirm them in their new faith. So even in the early days of the Church, the ideas of Baptism and Confirmation, or the "the laying on of hands," were key to becoming a Christian. In becoming confirmed you carry on a tradition that is truly as old as the Church itself.

"Now when the apostles at Jerusalem heard that Samaria had received the Word of God, they sent to them Peter and John, who came down and prayed for them that they might receive the Holy Spirit, for it had not yet fallen on any of them, but they had only been baptized in the name of the Lord Jesus. Then they laid their hands on them and they received the Holy Spirit." (Acts 8:14-17)

Very early in the history of the Church, those being confirmed also began to be anointed with a perfumed oil called "chrism" to better symbolize the gift of the Holy Spirit. Chrism is a word that is derived from "Christian," which means anointed, and from "Christ," whom God anointed with his Holy Spirit.

So when you are confirmed, you receive the Holy Spirit, just as Jesus did after his baptism, and just as the disciples did on the day of Pentecost. You are in very good company.

Why Do I Need the Holy Spirit?

"So what?" could be your response to all this stuff about Confirmation and the Holy Spirit. You might be thinking: "What difference does Confirmation make? I'll still be the same old person, won't I?"

Here are the most direct, honest answers to these two questions:

It CAN make a lot of difference.
No, you won't be the same old person, IF you choose to accept the sacrament in your heart and truly invite the Holy Spirit into your life.

When you receive the Holy Spirit, your life can be as dramatically changed as it was for the disciples on the first day of Pentecost. And just like your baptism, your Confirmation is a once-in-a-lifetime experience. God's seal, placed on you at Confirmation, will never go away. The Holy Spirit can:

bring you closer to God and to Jesus;
fill your life with a sense of meaning and purpose;
guide you through life;
help you make decisions; and
give you special strengths and gifts.

These special strengths will enable you to live a more fully Christian life. And like the disciples and prophets of old, you will be protected when you stand up for what you know is right and for what you know God wants you to do. Confirmation gives you the strength to be able to say boldly and proudly: "I am a Catholic. I am a Christian."

The special gifts the Spirit brings will help you live out your life as a Christian, too. These seven gifts help you:

● be wise;
● understand things and people better;
● give good advice;
● have courage;
● have knowledge;
● be reverent; and
● realize that God is awesome and full of wonder.

The Holy Spirit is given to those who ask. So by asking for and receiving the sacrament of Confirmation, you are asking for the Holy Spirit and all the gifts of the Spirit. That's a gift worth asking for.

"Guard what you have received. God the Father has marked you with his sign; Christ the Lord has confirmed you and has placed his pledge, the Spirit, in your hearts." *St. Ambrose*

"The Advocate, the Holy Spirit, whom the Father will send in my name, will teach you everything."
Jesus

"You will receive power when the Holy Spirit comes on you and then you will be my witnesses."
Jesus

"The Spirit came to help us in our weakness. For when we cannot choose words in order to pray properly, the Spirit expresses our plea in a way that could never be put into words." *St. Paul*

Why All the Classes? What's To Learn?

Remember: Being confirmed and joining the Church as a full member is like being selected for the "A" team. But before the season starts, you've got to get in shape! It's time to learn the plays, practice your skills, run those miles and do those hundreds and hundreds of sit ups.

Your preparation classes will do the same thing for you, leading you toward the beginning of your new life in the Church. Through these classes you will learn more about what it means to be a full member of the Church. You will learn about the responsibilities of Christian life. You will learn what it means to be a member of your parish church, your diocese and the worldwide Church of Jesus Christ.

But for you, this is also a time of questioning and doubt about many aspects of your life, including your faith and your Church. It's a time of searching. But the great thing is that you won't be searching and questioning alone. A big part of your preparation is getting to know

the others in your Confirmation class and experiencing what being part of a community is all about.

Just like most things in your life, what you learn and how well you learn it will be up to you, of course. But here's an idea of just some of things that you can learn during your preparation. You can learn:

- that you are called by name;
- about the signs and symbols associated with the sacrament;
- more about the significance of all the sacraments, but especially the Sacrament of Confirmation.
- more about the role and power of the Holy Spirit in your life and in the life of the Church.
- what it means to be a witness for Christ and live a Christian life.
- how to examine your own beliefs about God and the Church through questioning, challenging and exploring.

How to Go to Confession:
An Updated Guide

During your preparation for Confirmation, you'll also take a renewed look at the Sacrament of Reconciliation. This is a great opportunity to take a fresh look at God's law of love as revealed by Jesus Christ.

Jesus called people to follow him; to tell others the Good News that they are deeply loved by God, he will never reject them, they are special in his eyes. Our task as Christians and members of the Church is to preach this gospel (Good News) in the way we live and in and through our relationships.

In the sacrament of Reconciliation we are invited to reflect on whether we do accept the ways of Christ. Our sorrow for the times we have turned away from Christ can be faced in this sacrament. We acknowledge our failures and selfishness and are renewed in faith and hope.

We move on then, to an even closer relationship with Christ in and through reconciliation. If you have not been to confession for a while, here are a few tips to help prepare you for that long walk back to the confessional.

Take a deep breath. Then tell the priest what's going on in your life and what's been bothering you.

You're not 7 years old any more. Put aside the grocery list of sins and deal with the real things in your life for which you are sorry.

Get in touch with not just the sin but the reasons **why** you committed it. If you've missed Mass, ask yourself why.

Try to genuinely seek forgiveness and experience God's unconditional love. Know that God loves you no matter what.

Don't be vague about your failures. Name them so you know what you're dealing with.

There's no such thing as a free lunch. You are never taking action by just stopping. Try to replace a bad action with a good one.

Ask yourself this: What five words would I like to characterize me? Then ask: What's it going to take to make those words real? Finally, pray for the wisdom and courage to make it happen.

Time Out. I Have Some Questions...

No doubt you still have some questions about all of this. Here are some of your possible questions and their answers:

My parents were confirmed when they were really young. Why does the Church wait so long now?

Since your parents were confirmed there has been increasing flexibility in Church practice here. Confirmation is often considered the "sacrament of maturity" – a sign that you are truly ready to make decisions on your own about what you believe. The essential nature of the sacrament remains the same. The important point to remember is that the sacrament of Confirmation is the completion of your initiation as a Christian and it is also a confirmation that the Holy Spirit is active in your life, a sign that you have an important part to play in passing on the message that Christ gave to our world.

What if I don't get confirmed?

No one can make you get confirmed. If you choose not to receive this sacrament you leave your initiation incomplete. You reject the seal of the Spirit of Christ in your life which will enable you to live as a Christian in a more creative and dynamic way.

Should my parents force me to be confirmed?

If you don't want to get confirmed, then no one should force you. But remember, when the day of your Confirmation comes, it's up to you to receive the sacrament with an open heart.

Does everyone need to be confirmed?

Without Confirmation, your Christian initiation remains incomplete. Baptism, the Eucharist and the Sacrament of Confirmation together make up the "Sacraments of Christian Initiation." It's important you take advantage of all three of these sacraments, as together they bring you to full membership in the Church.

I have heard that I have to choose a Confirmation name. What's that all about?

Many people do decide to choose a Confirmation name; perhaps that of a saint who they particularly admire, but it isn't necessary. In fact, bearing in mind that your Confirmation is the completion of your initiation as a Christian it is an opportunity to reaffirm your baptismal name and so strengthen the connection in your own life between the moment you were first brought to Christ in baptism and this important celebration of your own confirmation in the faith.

I had a friend who died before being confirmed. What will happen to him?

As we say in the profession of faith, "We believe in one baptism for the forgiveness of sins." Being confirmed doesn't get you into heaven, so not being confirmed won't keep your friend from joining God in heaven. Confirmation is for the living. It is designed to bind the person more perfectly to the Church, to inspire us to reflect the life of Christ in our own lives and to bring him to others.

My parents don't go to church anymore. Why should I?

You decide to go to church or not for the same reason you decided to be confirmed – because you get to decide for yourself. When you are confirmed and become an adult in the eyes of the Church, you are even more responsible for the choices you make. Not going to church because your parents don't just doesn't make sense. Many people do things they shouldn't or don't do things that they should. You have to make your own decisions.

Confirmation: Would you do it all again?

"You bet," says a group of teenagers.

"Yes, it has taken me from a child who went to church to a man who goes to church." *Chris, 17*

"Yes, because anytime the Holy Spirit comes a mark is left on your soul." *Katie, 16*

"Yes, because it made me stronger in my faith and gave me a closer relationship with God." *Chuck, 15*

"Yes, I find truth in Christianity." *Steve, 16*

"Yes, I feel better about myself and my faith." *Anna, 15*

"Yes, because it got me involved with a lot of people, it brought me closer to my sponsor (my aunt), and closer to my Church." *Kelly, 14*

"Yes, it really made me feel closer to God and made me feel good."*Amy, 18*

"Yes, because it means a lot to me that I myself am accepting and wanting to be part of the Church."*Grainne, 16*

"Yes, there's nothing to lose and something to gain." *Luke, 15*

Your day of Confirmation is a day to celebrate. You'll probably buy new clothes, have a party and get presents. But the real action happens between you and the Spirit, and that's why the Church has a special celebration made just for this sacrament.

The Celebration of Confirmation

This may seem strange, but your Confirmation celebration actually starts a year ahead of time! Every year on Holy Thursday, your bishop consecrates the holy chrism (oil) for the whole diocese to use in the coming year. Usually, that same bishop will be the person presiding over your Confirmation, although at times he may empower your parish priest to perform the sacrament. Either way it's your special day.

The Sacrament of Confirmation is usually celebrated within the structure of the Mass, so many things will be familiar to you. There are the readings of the day and a homily by the bishop or priest. After you are confirmed you will go to Communion.

1

The Confirmation rite itself begins with the renewal of your baptismal promises, which originally were made for you by your parents and Godparents. The renewal of the promises is followed by your profession of faith. These two things at the beginning of the rite are your chance to stand on your own two feet and proclaim to everyone gathered that you really believe in what you are doing. It's also a chance for your parents and friends to renew their promises.

2

Next, the bishop extends his hands over the whole group of those being confirmed. Since the time of the apostles this gesture has symbolized the gift of the Holy Spirit. The bishop then uses these words to ask for the Holy Spirit to be poured out on all of you:

All-powerful God, Father of our Lord Jesus Christ,
by water and the Holy Spirit
you freed your sons and daughters from sin
and gave them new life.
Send your spirit upon them
to be their helper and guide.
Give them the spirit of wisdom and
  understanding,
the spirit of right judgment and courage,
the spirit of knowledge and reverence.
Fill them with the spirit of wonder and awe in
  your presence.
We ask this through Christ our Lord.

With these words you receive the Holy Spirit. If you really believe these words and hold them in your heart, your life will never be the same again.

3

Next you are anointed with the chrism. The bishop will make the sign of the cross with the chrism on your forehead, in much the same way you receive ashes on your forehead on Ash Wednesday. The bishop will then lay his hand on you and say these words: "Be sealed with the gift of the Holy Spirit."

4

The rite is concluded with a sign of peace between you and the bishop, symbolizing your communion with him and your full membership in the Church.

Chrism & Anointing

Just as historic documents often carry the seal of the crown or the seal of other important governing bodies, God places his seal on you at Confirmation to certify that you are real and that you belong to him. Oil is a symbol of abundance and joy. Some people put oil on themselves after bathing, and many athletes use oil to massage their sore muscles. Oil is also a sign of healing since it is soothing to bruises and wounds. It also glistens, which is why beauty queens and weight lifters often "anoint" themselves with oil—it makes their skin glisten.

Anointing with oil has all these meanings in the sacraments of the Church. Before you are baptized you were anointed with oil to symbolize cleansing and strengthening. The anointing of the sick and dying symbolizes healing and comfort. In Confirmation you are anointed with the sacred chrism as a sign of consecration—meaning you are joined to Christ. It's the same chrism used to consecrate new priests.

This seal says we belong to God forever and promise to serve the Church. In return, we acknowledge that God is our protector. That's why we can have the confidence to go to God in time of need. Because of this seal we know God is there for us.

Okay, It's Over. What Now?

"Young people, the world of today needs you, for it needs men and women who are filled with the Holy Spirit. It needs your courage and hopefulness, your faith and your perseverance. The world of tomorrow will be built by you."

Pope John Paul II

As you can see by the Pope's words, it is far from over. The Rite of Confirmation may be over, but your new life in the Spirit and in the Church is just beginning. You are a changed person. Here's what some teenagers had to say about how they have changed since confirmation:

I have greater respect for God.

I pray more often.

I became a better listener in church.

I have become closer to God.

My prayer life has become deeper and more intimate with God.

I have matured mentally.

I have really found out what confirmation is all about—choosing for myself.

I go to church more (I used to always have an excuse).

I've become a better person.

I've realized the true meaning of my faith.

I feel more a part of the Church.

I feel it's now easier to talk to God.

My faith has strengthened.

I'm more responsible.

I have realized what confirmation means and have accepted my responsibilities in the Church.

I'm more thoughtful and appreciative of the things going on around me.

I've grown in self-confidence and generally matured.

I've become an individual ready to stand up

and profess my beliefs.

I try to think more about the meaning of being a Christian.

I'm happier than I've ever been, knowing God is always with me.

I now understand what the Holy Spirit is and how powerful it can be.

Making Good Decisions

Just as Confirmation is all about "making a decision," much of your life after Confirmation has to do with making decisions. Face it. The choices you make and the decisions you face as teenagers can be life-changing. Whether you realize it or not, you make choices every day that deeply affect your life and the lives of those around you. You've got two choices when it comes to making choices. You can decide for yourself and have control of your life, or you can let the decisions decide themselves and take what the roll of the dice gives you. Here are a few suggestions for making your next all-important decision:

- State the decision to be made clearly.

- List the pros and cons of the situation. Be truthful.

- List the possible effects your decision could have on you, your friends, and your family.

- Ask a friend or someone you trust what he or she thinks. Remember that God works through others, and he may be speaking to you through a friend.

- Take it to God. Pray for help in your decision, and then be sure to listen and watch for a response. An answer may not come out of the clouds, but God has ways of getting through.

Dear God,
Thank you for the great gift you have
given me in the Sacrament of
Confirmation.
Thank you for sending the Holy
Spirit into my life to offer me
guidance and help.
I ask for that guidance now, Lord.
I need to know where I fit into this
Church of yours.
What am I to do? What do I have to
offer? Where am I to serve?
I have so many questions right now.
Be with me on my journey of faith,
Lord.
Give me patience to wait for your
answers.
Give me an open heart to hear you
when you respond.
Give me your love and forgiveness,
for I know I will make mistakes
along the way.
Amen.

A New View of the Church

As a full member of the Catholic Church now, you will soon realize that there are many roles that need to be filled if the Church is to "work." Perhaps you took many of these for granted in the past, but now the responsibility for making the Church work is as much your responsibility as it is your parents', your teachers' and even your parish priests'. Where do you fit in? What are your gifts? What can you offer?

There is not one answer, of course. But over time and through prayer, you can come to find your place in the Church. That's the most important thing you can do right now—begin searching for and praying about your role. You can use the prayer above as a starting point.

Some Final Words For the Journey...

Don't just take our word for it. Here's what some teenagers would like to tell you about confirmation:

"It is an experience unlike any other because it fills you in so many ways. It makes you an adult of the Church, so in a way it can make you feel more trusted and responsible. It can boost your self-esteem." *Karen, 17*

"When you get confirmed you are finally considered an adult in the eyes of the Church. So this is a big step in your life." *Chris, 17*

"I think you should get confirmed because you will be following in the traditions of the Church and will have completed your steps from Baptism to Confirmation." *Katie, 16*

"When you get confirmed you feel closer to God and you feel you have a more important role in the Church." *Tom, 15*

"This is probably the first and most important real choice you will make." *Steve, 16*

"I would have to say that the Spirit will definitely guide you and you will definitely feel more 'grown up' in the Church." *Anna, 15*

"It brings you closer to the Holy Spirit. You can feel the Spirit's presence easier. You are more free in the Church because you make your own decisions." *Shelley, 17*

"It helps you become closer to God and helps you grow in your faith." *Pam, 19*

"It's a great accomplishment; a 'step up' in the Church. You're becoming a member of something good." *Tiffany, 18*

"It's your decision. Do it because you believe in it." *Elizabeth, 15*

"Becoming a member of the Church is a very special commitment, and by letting the Holy Spirit into your life, the Spirit will help you understand the true meaning of God." *Michael, 17*

"It is an important decision that must be thought about. It means you want to become a full member of the Church, like your parents." *Grainne, 16*

"You receive the Holy Spirit. That will stay with you for the rest of your life." *Anna, 17*

"Even if you don't really think that it means much at this stage in your life, you will get a lot of meaning out of it when you come to different stages in your life, such as your teenage years. If you have made your confirmation it's easier to accept and follow your religion, and you can consider God to be more of a friend in times of trouble. And believe me, there are plenty of times when you are growing up when you really need God." *Lou, 16*

"Do it because it's what you want – otherwise don't bother. Do it because you have thought it through and want to publicly declare your beliefs and invite and accept God's Holy Spirit into your life." *Liz, 16*

"It gives you the chance to let the Holy Spirit into your life." *Matt, 16*

"You become a member of a welcoming community—the Catholic faith. You receive the gift of the Holy Spirit, which is an honour." *Kim, 16*

"It might change your life for the better. It can't change it for the worse, but it just might give you something valuable." *Chris, 17*